Noisy Stones

A Meditation Manual

Robert R. Walsh

Boston

Skinner House Books

© 1992 by Robert R. Walsh. All rights reserved. Published by Skinner House Books, an imprint of the Unitarian Universalist Association, 25 Beacon Street, Boston, MA 02108-2800.

ISBN 1-55896-247-6

Printed in the USA.

Design by Suzanne Morgan

We are grateful for the excerpt on p. 12 from Carl Sandburg's "Prayers of Steel," taken from *The Complete Poems of Carl Sandburg*, Harcourt Brace Jovanovich, Inc., © 1918 by Holt, Rinehart and Winston, Inc.; © 1946 by Carl Sandburg; © 1969, 1970 by Lilian Steichen Sandburg, Trustee. The meditation entitled "The Divine Secret" is based on a passage from James Martineau's *Endeavors After the Christian Life* (1834).

Walsh, Robert R. 1937-
    Noisy stones: a meditation manual/Robert R. Walsh.
        p. cm.
        1. Meditations.   I. Title.
    BL624.2.W35 1992
    242—dc20
                                                91-37430
                                                CIP

To
Con Browne
Jim Curtis
Arthur Graham
Manuel "Dutch" Holland
Ernie Howard
Ken MacLean
and
Bob Palmer

who first taught me about ministry.

Contents

Preface

At the noisy, abrasive margin of earth and sea and sky, I pick up shiny beach stones to carry home. Like the ideas that started these meditations, the stones always take the initiative— saying, *notice me*. In my quiet study, the beach stones I've collected are no longer shaped by the world's friction. Here, instead, I shape the ideas so that I may give them to you.

If this book has a theme, it is this: surprises. Here are surprises that have come my way as I have gone about the work of ministry in a Unitarian Universalist parish. Here, especially, is the surprising gift of this day. Notice it! Shape it!

For advice and encouragement, I'm grateful to Elizabeth Tarbox, Carol Egan, Peter Fleck, Forrest Church, and Brendan Hanlon. Thanks to Emily Caleskie for patience and good humor, and to the people of the First Parish Church in Duxbury for being a forgiving community through eleven years of learning the parish ministry. And, finally, thanks to Reed Walsh for steady and loving companionship and support.

Robert R. Walsh

Katahdin Incident

On a summer day I hiked with my fifteen-year-old son through the Maine wilderness toward the north basin of Mt. Katahdin. We had found time for the outing in the brief interval between my summer job as a chaplain and the beginning of my second year at Harvard Divinity School.

The August sun beat down out of a clear sky. We took a short side trail and came upon a large pond. The still water was like blue tinted crystal. Around the perimeter of the pond were bare white stones. Beyond the stones were dense dark green trees. The sky was a deep blue. In the distance we could see the sheer rock cliffs of the north face of Katahdin. With our backs to the mouth of the trail we could see no evidence that the human race had ever inhabited the planet.

Then two hikers approached. They were young men— tan, muscular, bearded, sweaty. They were carrying backpacks, and I guessed they had been on the trail for several days.

The first hiker fixed his gaze on the pond. With smooth motions he laid down his pack, slipped off his boots and socks, and peeled off his T-shirt as he walked toward the water. I knew exactly what he was about to do.

He reached for his belt buckle, then turned toward my son and me and spoke for the first time. He said, "I hope you're not offended by nudity."

I shrugged and said, "It doesn't bother me."

As he pulled off his pants he said, "Well, you never know when there might be a preacher in the crowd."

One Morning in Marshfield

The early morning call was from the Marshfield Police Department. There had been a death. The family was vacationing; they had no connections in town. None of the clergy in Marshfield could be reached.

It was a two-story house across the street from the ocean wall. A red-eyed woman met me at the screen door and invited me in without waiting for an introduction. Several people of different ages sat quietly in the kitchen. The police officer said softly that she had died during the night. She is upstairs; you can go on up. I asked her name. Annie.

Then I was alone with her, as they had found her that morning: the mother, mother-in-law, aunt, and grandmother of the people downstairs. I said, "Hello, Annie." I touched her hand. What did they want me to do?

As I came downstairs the doctor arrived. He went up to examine the body, came back down, interviewed some of the people in the kitchen, filled out a form. I sat alone in the living room.

The funeral director arrived. He interviewed some of the people in the kitchen, returned to his vehicle, brought back a complex mechanical stretcher. The police officer offered to help. They soon came down the steep stair with the body wrapped in a blanket and strapped to the stretcher. They took it to the black station wagon. The police officer left. The funeral director left. The doctor left.

The family came out of the kitchen and joined me in the living room. I asked them to tell me about Annie, and they did.

As I drove home, I envied those other three professionals. They had known exactly what to do.

Autumn Alert

I have just returned from the northern woods and I bring alarming news. Something there is turning the leaves to red and gold . . . and it's coming this way.

Already here one can see signs. An unfamiliar coolness in the air. Sailboats being brought in. Just this morning a school bus went by.

Take warning, friends. Every leaf in our fair town is doomed, and every green unfinished summer dream will now be foreclosed. We have had our fleeting summertime.

A Man's Prayer

I am wondrously wrought: partly shaped by my biology, partly shaped by my culture, and partly self-shaped.

I am so wonderfully fashioned that the workings of my self amaze and confuse me.

I know I have the power to choose among many paths, yet most of the time I am on automatic pilot, acting out of little-examined assumptions, values, rituals, myths, appetites, and impulses.

I can meet life in many ways:

I can be tough-minded; I can be tender-hearted.

I can move between activity and quietness.

I can express my uniqueness and individuality, and I can forget myself in commitment to family and community.

I can judge, I can bear witness to the good and the evil around me; and I can forgive.

I can analyze, theologize, figure the world out; and I can listen to the still small voice of conscience, intuition, the holy spirit.

All these ways of meeting life, and more, are part of the potential that is me. But I am afraid to move very far or very fast from the ways that have become comfortable.

I seek the self-knowledge that may illuminate new possibilities in life, and I seek the courage to try them.

Most of all I pray for wholeness, for a life in which my many ways of living can be connected and filled with the meaning of holy Creation.

Gathering

When we tell the story of our church we say it was gathered in 1632. Most institutions are not described as having been gathered. Corporations and banks, hospitals and universities, put up oil paintings called *Our Founder*. If we had a picture of the pilgrims who started our church, we could call it *Our Gatherers*.

"Founding" sounds vertical, linear. It sounds masculine, or even fatherly. We build a firm foundation; we lay a cornerstone; we look to the future, which we expect to move us onward and upward. "Found" comes from a Latin word meaning "bottom." So when we found something we are making a bottom for it, a bottom on which it will later stand.

To "gather" sounds horizontal and circular and timeless. It sounds earthy, close to nature—not something you do with a cement mixer or a backhoe, but something you do with a basket. Founding focuses on the future, but gathering is of this season. If founding fathers mark the beginning of a hierarchy, gatherers come together in equality.

The Bible is full of images of founding. An indignant God demands of Job, "Where were you when I laid the foundation of the earth?" Jesus, speaking from within this tradition, says, "Upon this rock I will build my church." But elsewhere, breaking out of this tradition, he says, "For where two or three are gathered in my name, there am I in the midst of them."

We are a community of gatherers and founders. Neither is sufficient; both are necessary. Welcome to those who are layers of cornerstones, and to those who are gatherers of grain, or rosebuds, or moss, or momentum, or congregations.

The Timeless Lunch

I had lunch with a person who had just passed her second birthday. Her vocabulary included ketchup, salt, pickle, mustard, and spoon—but she could not yet name the Worcestershire sauce. She could count to ten with confidence— but when she got into the teens she began to rattle off numbers at random. Her curiosity was boundless. I knew that her knowledge of the world would grow apace, and her ability to manipulate the symbols of language would expand.

I thought, the little person I see before me, lining up the restaurant condiments and counting and naming them, exists only for this moment. Even in the course of this meal she is growing and changing. If I meet her again in a month, she will be learning something else, and saying other words. She—and I—will have left this day behind.

I knew that the moment I had across the table from her was irreplaceable. There could be no other meeting between that particular her and that particular me. The experience could not be saved up or stored. So I was there with her as she spooned milk into the mouth of her stuffed bear.

And I think I loved her, when she held my hand as her mother unlocked the car.

Returning from Jordan Hospital, Early October

The red leaves shouted. I don't know how long
they worked at getting my attention. Eyes
on striped macadam, aimless thoughts of pain
and death and illness, issues of the self,
and selfless prayer—or was it just a wish?—
I blocked the sight without the aid of shades
or blinders.
        When the brightness hit me I
was stunned, a blow right to the soul, a K.O.
to the spiritual solar plexus. Here
was transformation, all creation, in
its work ongoing, all around me. And
destruction, too, and death (forget them at
your peril). Eddying, splashing entropy
was running to the sea.
           A rest stop sign
appeared and I pulled off the road where I
could safely cry.

Acquitted of Universalism

In the newspaper there was a story about a seminary professor in Kansas City who was put on trial by the Southern Baptists, accused of being a universalist.

It's no wonder they were suspicious. He had stated publicly his belief that all people born into the world are children of God.

And as if that were not enough, he also supported the ordination of women. Case closed?

The professor denied the charges. "I'm not a universalist," he said, and he convinced them. After four hours of deliberation they voted 21 to 11 to let him keep his job.

Now, I confess to being a universalist. In fact, I am a Unitarian Universalist. But I wonder. If I were arrested and charged with being one, would there be enough evidence to convict me?

The Kansas City story proves that having the right beliefs is not enough. The professor believed that all people are brothers and sisters, that every person has a piece of the divine spark, that women are the equals of men in the sight of God. That was not enough to bring in a guilty verdict.

No, if they are going to pin Unitarian Universalism on me they will have to be able to show that I participated in and supported a Unitarian Universalist church. That is the only way to be sure. Beliefs, no matter how noble, must be embodied in a living institution or they will have no convicting power.

Does Generosity Cause Happiness?

A colleague told me he had read in a magazine that people who are generous with their money are happier, suffer fewer headaches, and have better sex lives.

Here it is, I thought, the keys to the kingdom for the 1990s. Tithe and be saved—on earth at least.

I spent about an hour and a half going through old magazines until I found the article. Alas, the information was inaccurate. The article reports that people who enjoy *spending* money are happier, suffer fewer headaches, and have better sex lives.

So we are back to the old arguments for giving to the church. The rewards we get from giving may be less tangible than those we get from spending, but they are no less real.

But then, who knows? Maybe generosity has the same effect as extravagance. Maybe your generous pledge to the church will help you with those headaches.

Something Will Grow

How do these things work? Can anyone
explain this movement, this new greenness here?
A boy at chapel handed me three bulbs
at rest on gravel in a Cool Whip tub.
I'm in a church school project now, I thought.
Something will grow. I knew that this would happen,
see? I put it on the shelf.
                                    Then they
began to move. Three green projections pierced
the bulbous tops. I moved them to my desk
so as not to miss the show. But one gets busy.

Quite without my noticing, the green
projections grew still longer, till
I saw them standing high above the jumble,
unaffected by the flow of cares
across the desk. On up and out of crinkled
bulbs into the room of air the green
shoots grew. They bent to seek the light. I set
them by the window.
                                    And I thought, these green
things in my office grow and move about
when I'm not here. They telescoped way up
from balls of onion shape. And I don't know
what makes them work.
                                    And now three clusters of
white petals blossom from the shoots. They're looking
out the window toward the fallen leaves.

Assignment

While I am away, here are some things I want you to do. I want you to take care of yourself. Button up your overcoat. Fasten your seat belt. Eat your vegetables.

I want you to take care of someone else. Look for ways to help. Say, "I love you" (if you do). Hug a friend.

I want you to take care of your soul. Keep the different parts of your self in touch with one another. Listen for quiet clues about the path your life should be following. Be aware of what kind of world you are helping to make each day.

Take good care.

Divine Crowbars

Lay me on an anvil, O God.
Beat me and hammer me into a crowbar.
Let me pry loose old walls.
Let me lift and loosen old foundations.

Carl Sandburg asks to become a crowbar in the hands of God, wedge and fulcrum applied to cracks in old mortar, sending bricks crumbling.

We do not usually depict God as doing demolition work. But when there's a wall that imprisons people, or a foundation that destroys the human spirit, then some of us need to become divine crowbars.

In the nations of Eastern Europe masses of people have taken risks for freedom. Wedges have been inserted into the cracks of totalitarianism. An old wall (a real one) has been pried loose.

There is something in the creation that wants to move toward liberation and away from oppression. It does not always prevail, but it is always at work. It was told of in the ancient stories and in this morning's newspaper.

Let us look for other walls and foundations that need lifting and loosening. There are structures in our lives that keep us from becoming the people we might be. There are human spirits being crushed by walls and foundations we have helped build and maintain.

We need some demolition, too. Can you become a crowbar?

Pop's Prayer

My earliest memory of a prayer is the table grace my grandfather used to say. I associate it with holiday meals, with extended family crowded around a long dining room table. I remember the smell of turkey gravy, the sight of bowed heads—and then the gruff voice of this old man delivering the prayer as if it were one long word accented on the first and last syllables: "*Lord*makeusthankfulfortheseprovisionsweaskinchristsake*amen*."

The last word sounded like "gah-*men!*" I thought that was the way one ended a prayer.

I remember years when I had no idea what he was saying. The prayer had meaning that did not depend on knowing. It was an invocation for the larger liturgy of the meal. Its meanings, beyond language, had to do with bonds: my bonds to the food, my parents and sister, the aunts and uncles and cousins and grandparents there, the warmth of the room, the celestial and human rhythms that brought us to that table, and other mysteries beyond these.

There came a time when I figured out the words to Pop's prayer, but that did not seem to affect its meaning. It was much, much later, after turning this memory over until it was worn smooth, that I realized something important about the prayer. I had thought it was a prayer of thanksgiving. But Pop did not say, "Lord, thank you." He said, "Lord, make us thankful." It was a prayer of petition.

We were beginning those special meals, not with thanks for the bountiful gifts before us and around us, but with a confession that we were not thankful enough. "Make us thankful." Wake us up. Our gratitude is dulled by the very abundance of what we have. Bring us, somehow, to enough clarity of vision to see what a miracle is this creation in which we find ourselves.

In truth, we are not thankful enough: a confession with which to begin our thanksgiving. Gah-*men!*

Fire at the Parsonage

The fire started about midnight Saturday in the little storage room that connects the kitchen to the garage. To look into that burning room was to glimpse another world, a surprising alternate universe. It had always been an ordinary room I could walk in and out of, or through to the other side, without anything unusual happening. I was familiar with the contents of the room. I knew the texture and color of its surfaces. It had a certain smell and a certain sound.

This time when I opened the door I saw flames and swirling smoke that moved toward me and past me and stung my eyes and burned the inside of my nose. The universe had been orderly. Now, flowing out of that room into the rest of the world was chaos. Things were out of control. Destructive forces were loose.

The chief difference between the universe before and the universe after the opening of that door was in the dimension of time. I well know that all the things to which I am connected, loved ones, favored possessions, self, will be swept away in time. But the fire said: now. It may happen now.

The world is going to end, and we don't know when. My world, or yours, may end tomorrow in some unexpected way. Our shared world, earth's biosphere, will end as well; maybe ten million years from now when the sun overheats; maybe next week in an accidental nuclear war. We may have no warning, no time to prepare. Have we done what we need to do? Have we said the words we should say before the opportunity is gone?

The walls are cool now. The charred and water-soaked things are piled outside. The urgency has been replaced by weariness and aggravation. I remember that for a while I thought I knew exactly what was most important.

Fault Line

Did you ever think there might be a fault line
passing underneath your living room:
a place in which your life is lived in meeting
and in separating, wondering
and telling, unaware that just beneath
you is the unseen seam of great plates
that strain through time? And that your life, already
spilling over the brim, could be invaded,
sent off in a new direction, turned
aside by forces you were warned about
but not prepared for? Shelves could be spilled out,
the level floor set at an angle in
some seconds' shaking. You would have to take
your losses, do whatever must be done
next.
     When the great plates slip
and the earth shivers and the flaw is seen
to lie in what you trusted most, look not
to more solidity, to weighty slabs
of concrete poured or strength of cantilevered
beam to save the fractured order. Trust
more the tensile strands of love that bend
and stretch to hold you in the web of life
that's often torn but always healing. There's
your strength. The shifting plates, the restive earth,
your room, your precious life, they all proceed
from love, the ground on which we walk together.

The Minister Goes for Help

Among the programs I have for my personal computer is one that will talk with me about my problems. It's a software pastoral counselor. The name of the program is Eliza.

Saturday night I was feeling troubled and I called Eliza up on the screen. She always opens the session the same way. She says, "How do you do? Please tell me your problem." I typed in, "What is the true meaning of Christmas?"

E: Why do you ask?

R: People expect me to know the answer.

E: I am not sure I understand you fully.

R: I am a minister and I want to explain the meaning of Christmas in a sermon.

E: Is it because you are a minister and you want to explain the meaning of Christmas in a sermon that you came to me?

R: That's right.

E: Can you expand on that?

In the trade we call this "non-directive counseling."

Given this invitation, I explained that Christmas is a major preoccupation of many people at this time of year, that it is both a religious occasion and a secular occasion, that both the religious and the secular celebrations are thousands of years old and have roots in several ancient traditions and have layers upon layers of meanings that have been added over the centuries and that the religious and the secular parts of the occasion are all mixed up with each other and as a result it is a complicated event. And I explained that some of us worry that the superficial meanings, the easy meanings, the profitable meanings that crowd us in our seasonal rush are obscuring a deeper and essential meaning of Christmas that we must hold on to if we can.

E: Do you think it's likely that we can?

R: We can if we will take the time to pause and to become aware.

E: Do you wish that we will take the time to pause and to become aware?

R: You're just repeating what I say.

E: What makes you think I am just repeating what you say?

R: Oh, forget it.

E: Can you expand on that?

R: Let's get back to the true meaning of Christmas.

E: I am not sure I understand you fully.

R: This is where I came in.

E: You say this is where you came in?

R: Goodbye.

E: Goodbye. That will be $75, please.

Quest for Marmalade

Before we went to Scotland I made a short list of the things I wanted to see. Edinburgh. Some of those bleak Scottish castles. Inverness, Loch Ness, and the Highlands. Loch Lomond. And I wanted to see where they make Dundee marmalade. I wanted to bring home a jar of Dundee marmalade that I had bought in Dundee.

Dundee marmalade was one of those critical discoveries I made in college—like Faulkner, the Second Law of Thermodynamics, beer, Scollay Square, Frank Lloyd Wright, lobster, and folk music.

It was delicious stuff, and it came in an unforgettable package: a jar with a baked glazed white finish, with the product information printed on it in smudged black ink, and a lid made of . . . paper! On the jar it said, "James Keiller & Son, Ltd. Dundee Marmalade Est. 1797," and on the lid (I think) it said, "By Appointment to His Majesty King Something-or-Other." We would save the jars and keep pencils in them. I've got two of them on my desk right now.

So we went to Dundee, and as things turned out we didn't have time to look for the James Keiller & Son, Ltd. factory. But I went into a market to look for the marmalade. I was stunned to discover that among the jams and preserves there was not a single jar of anything made in Dundee, or anything bearing the Keiller name.

A few days later I read in the *Edinburgh Scotsman* that whatever remained of James Keiller & Son had just been sold by one large corporation to another and that the seventeen employees who were still on marmalade were to be switched to making candied jelly babies.

So my quest was fruitless, and we returned from our travels without the one item I had hoped to bring back. But at Christmas we found under the tree a fresh new jar of Dundee marmalade, a gift from the first Parish Church Sewing Group, whose members had heard me tell this story. It turns out you can buy Dundee marmalade at the Stop & Shop in Pembroke, Massachusetts—but not in Dundee. The marmalade was very good.

Lo, the Star

Here is something very few people know about. There are many wonderful times in a year of being a parish minister, but there is nothing that quite compares with a certain moment toward the end of the Christmas pageant. There before me is the babe nestled in straw; around him are his parents, shepherds, angels, a variety of friendly beasts; three oriental monarchs are slowly advancing down the center aisle; hundreds of people watch quietly by candlelight. I read, "They departed; and lo, the star which they saw in the east went before them." Over my head suddenly shines . . . the star!

I get turned on as much as the star, and I'm not sure why. Is it the drama? Is it the surprise, which I imagine that only I know is coming? Is it the power of an epiphany, the divine presence breaking through into the world? Is it the momentary illusion of control—that heavenly bodies respond to my word? (My word!)

Anyway, this was the year the star didn't go on at the right time. I experienced a technical difficulty. Upon the intonation of "lo," I pushed the little switch in my right hand, but over my head the light did not shine.

I recovered quickly. At the end of verse eleven ("gold, frankincense, and myrrh") I glanced over my shoulder, confirmed my worst suspicions, and pressed the switch through another cycle. And then the people who sat in darkness saw a great light.

This is a moral tale, and here are its lessons. First, my control over the cosmos, or much of anything else, is indeed an illusion. Second, things often turn out well in spite of my inability to control them. Third, if the divine presence breaks through, the timing is up to it and not to me—and the best I can do is to stay loose enough to be open to it.

A New Year

I once actually greeted the new year in Times Square. It was the beginning of 1954, when I was sixteen. We stayed at the Hotel Taft. The orchestra of Vincent Lopez was playing in the Taft ballroom, and I danced with my mother. Times Square was cold, crowded, brightly lit, noisy, and exciting. People spoke to strangers and wished them well. At midnight I was at the center of the world and at the center of time. I had no sense of fear in Times Square.

I remember feeling that the discontinuity at the turn of the year was real, that time stopped at midnight and then started again, that the new year with its new number was really new.

Now my parents are gone, Vincent Lopez is gone, Times Square has become a different kind of place, and to my grown-up instincts the city at midnight brings a sense of danger. I have danced and sung and hugged and kissed through many a New Year's Eve. I have made new beginnings, good ones, although I think none of them happened on a January 1st.

I wish for you in this new year as many new beginnings as you need, and no more than you can handle. May they come not at a particular turn of the calendar page or striking of the clock, but just when you need them.

In this year, may you remember old acquaintances, and may peace break out, even if only a little bit, in the world, and in your life.

It Matters

I knew a man who had printed on his stationery this proverb: "Nothing is settled. Everything matters." It established a certain ambience for reading his letters, as if to say: what you are about to read is to be taken seriously, but is not final.

I remember him and his proverb sometimes, especially when it seems impossible to change the world or myself in any significant way. Times like the beginnings of new years.

"Sorry, Jim," I say. "It's not true that nothing is settled. In the past year choices have been made, losses have been suffered, there has been growth and decay, there have been commitments and betrayals. None of that can be undone. A year ago no one knew whether during this year one person would become pregnant, another would get cancer, another would take a new job, another would have an accident, but now it is settled.

"One day this year I was present just when someone needed me; another day I was busy doing something else when I was needed. One day I said something to a friend that injured our relationship; another day I said something that enabled a person to see life in a new way. The best and the worst of those days is now written. All my tears, of joy or sorrow, cannot erase it."

If I stay with my meditation long enough, the reply comes. "Robbie," says Jim, "You have misunderstood the proverb. It is true that you cannot escape the consequences of your actions or the chances of the world. But what is not settled is how the story turns out. What is not settled is what the meaning of your life will be."

The meaning of a life is not contained within one act, or one day, or one year. As long as you are alive the story of your life is still being told, and the meaning is still open. As long as there is life in the world, the story of the world is still being told. What is done is done, but *nothing is settled*.

And if nothing is settled, then *everything matters*. Every choice, every act in the new year matters. Every word, every deed is making the meaning of your life and telling the story of the world. Everything matters in the year coming, and, more important, everything matters today.

A Good Age

I don't mind being fifty. It seems a good age to me. There is much joking around big birthdays in mid-life, but there's often a sick quality to it. It is humor that plays off a fear of aging. This is the dominant theme in humorous birthday cards. The people who manufacture these cards know what they're doing: they're capitalizing on a fear that is deep in our collective psyche.

We would enjoy life a lot more if we could accept the things that are given and just worry about the things we can influence. What does it profit us to deny our age?

Don't get me wrong—I grieve over the losses I have suffered in the passing of time. I am angry and frustrated about the parts of my body that don't work as well as they used to. For example, my eyes. Oh, for the days when, unassisted, I could read my digital wristwatch and then look up and read a distant traffic sign!

But needing bifocals and being fifty are two different things. They may go together, they may not. Some people are born with poor eyesight, and some never need glasses. Loss of good vision is bad, but being fifty is good.

So let us try to eat properly and exercise and get enough sleep and stay interested in the world. Let us rage at the losses of family and friends and muscle tone and organic functioning, and at the pain. But let us realize that it is good, very good, to be exactly the age we are.

A Nonalogue for the Fridge

A friend asked me to try my hand at rewriting the Ten Commandments. She wanted something to tape to the door of the fridge.

I only came up with nine. But then I spent much less time on this than it took Moses to climb the mountain.

1. You shall not worship the finite and the conditional as if it were the ultimate.

2. You shall keep to a rhythm of work and rest in the spirit of the sabbath.

3. You shall keep your promises.

4. You shall tell the truth.

5. You shall try to make amends for the things you break.

6. You shall honor the people who give and sustain life.

7. You shall honor the earth.

8. You shall grant to others the same rights to life, liberty, and property that you claim for yourself.

9. You shall be kind.

Warning from the Steamship Authority

I emptied my pockets at the end of the day and found among the coins and keys a small piece of paper that read: "NOT VALID IF DETACHED." It was a stub from a ferry boat ticket.

Not valid if detached. Is it true? Maybe not. Detachment can be valuable. Sometimes it is important to get a detached view. A person who is detached, and therefore objective, is a more reliable witness in a court of law. A juror might say, "Not valid *unless* detached."

It is possible to become so attached to a person or a cause that we cannot distinguish our own issues from those of another. In such a relationship we may not take care of ourselves. A measure of detachment under such circumstances can be healing for all concerned. We might even say, "*More* valid if *more* detached."

Still, I want to listen to the warning on the ticket stub, for being detached can also mean being indifferent. Being objective about another person may make it possible to treat that person as an object. Being detached from the world or any of its parts can make it easier for us to avoid our responsibility for it.

To strike a member of our family we must first be detached. To permit our teenage children to have unchaperoned drinking parties in our homes we must be detached. We must be detached if we are to paint a swastika on a synagogue, tell a disparaging joke about gay people, cut public health care and nutrition programs for poor children, or drop bombs on a civilian neighborhood in Panama City.

It is only through our detachment that we are able to rend the ozone layer, poison the air and the sea, exterminate whole species of animals, and burn the rain forests.

There are times when some detachment is appropriate and necessary. But the greatest source of evil in our time may be that we are too detached from people, and too detached from the

earth. If we meet everything objectively, then there is no sacred-
ness and no mystery.

Listen to the warning.

These Stones Do Not Lack Interest

These stones do not lack interest even though
their passive presence on the dresser top
awaits initiative from me. They go
for weeks without the least attention.

These stones have pleasing rounded shapes,
their quiet colors uniform or varied.
Some have faded stripes or circles, some
are spotted. Some are intersected by
contrasting seams of other kinds of rock.
One white stone has a cross of black. And one
looks like a cream cheese sandwich.

These stones have got integrity. They rest
in dryness of the air, on smoothness of
the wood, in incandescent light, presenting
grainy surfaces that are exactly
what they seem to be.
                      The stones
I picked up weren't like this.

Motions of the tides had brought them to
the great margin of earth and sea and sky.
The stones I chose from all the others showed
me surfaces that shone with cold fire.

I was the passive one. Each one of these
commanded me to pause. The colors came
as if from deep within: the shining yellows,

glowing ochres, whites as pure as any
pearl, the rings like bands of Jupiter,
the blacks as black as space between the stars.

And now they rest, in isolation, dusty,
far removed from forces that gave them
their form. I have interrupted for
a while their evolution toward becoming
sand grains.
                    But I remember when
I plucked them from the great margin. I
remember seeing them in moving noisy
bright abrasive wetness. How they shone!

More Than We Deserve

I heard the Second Brandenburg Concerto played in honor of Bach's 300th birthday, and I was swept away. I remembered a story about the people who send messages into outer space. Someone suggested sending a piece by Bach. The reply was: "But that would be bragging."

Some say we get what we deserve in life, but I don't believe it. We certainly don't deserve Bach. What have I done to deserve the Second Brandenburg Concerto? I have not been kind enough; I have not done enough justice; I have not loved my neighbor, or myself, sufficiently; I have not praised God enough to have earned a gift like this.

Life is a gift we have not earned and for which we cannot pay. There is no necessity that there be a universe, no inevitability about a world moving toward life and then self-consciousness. There might have been . . . nothing at all.

Since we have not earned Bach—or crocuses or lovers—the best we can do is express our gratitude for the undeserved gifts, and do our share of the work of creation.

A Baptism

She called to ask if I would baptize her infant son.

I said, "What we do is like a baptism, but not exactly. And we normally do it only for people who are part of the church family. The next one we have scheduled is in May."

She said, "Could we come to talk with you about it anyway?"

They came to see me, the very young woman and her child and the child's very young father.

She explained that the child had been born with a heart defect. He had to have a risky heart operation soon. She had asked the clergyman of her own church if he would baptize her son, and he had refused because she was not married to the baby's father.

I told them that their not being married would not be an impediment to anything we might do, but that our child dedication ceremony still might not be what they were looking for.

I explained that our ceremony does not wash away any sin, it does not guarantee the child a place in heaven, it doesn't even make the child a member of the church.

In fact, I said, it doesn't change the child at all. What we expect is that it will change the rest of us in our relationship with the child, and with all children.

She listened patiently.

When I was through she said, "All I want is to know that God blesses my baby."

In my mind I gasped at the sudden clarity in the room.

I said, with a catch in my throat, "I think I can do that."

And I did.

No Hell

No hell!" cried the Universalists. Their movement was named for the heresy of believing that a loving God would not condemn any soul to eternal punishment. The idea of universal salvation was shocking two centuries ago, but deeply appealing to people raised on religions of fear. The Universalists flourished. Later, their movement waned as other denominations softened their images of fire and brimstone.

It does not shock today to say there is no hell. Yet, the idea of hell persists. Some say the reason it has such staying power is that the churches need it to keep people in line. I think it goes deeper.

I think the idea of hell stays with us because we are terrified that the Ground of Being might include both good and evil, both justice and injustice, destruction as well as creation, death as well as life. We have created such symbols as Satan, the lake of fire, and the subtle serpent to isolate and neutralize the threatening side of God.

We hold on to hell because when we discard it we glimpse through the clearing smoke a God who is too complicated for us.

Omne Vivum Ex Ovo

A friend stopped me at the post office and told me that at the moment of the vernal equinox it is possible to stand eggs up on their ends. I looked up the time in the almanac and set my alarm. At 5:03 p.m. I was home, in the kitchen, with the eggs beside me. I stood three of them up on the smooth ceramic cutting board. I called my wife in to witness it. At 5:07 one of them rolled over, but I stood it back up again. They stayed there until about 5:25, when we got tired of watching them and put them away.

The next day I saw my friend again. She said she just saw on the television that the story about the eggs was a hoax.

Solvents

They've discovered that Michelangelo originally painted the Sistine Chapel ceiling in bright colors, and some people are upset about it.

When we visited the Vatican they were about three-quarters through with the big cleaning job on the ceiling. The restorers were working from a bridge-like scaffold designed much like Michelangelo's, using the same mounting holes in the walls. As the cleaning was done, the scaffold was moved down the length of the ceiling. The movement was in reverse primordial time, starting with the flood and moving toward the creation.

Someone said the scaffold was like a very slow windshield wiper. In front of it the frescoes were dull and gloomy. Behind it they were clear and bold. We were among the first people in several centuries to see those bright colors. The almost-touching fingers of God and Adam were just visible on the clean side of the scaffold. It looked wonderful.

There are art critics who claim that Michelangelo was a gloomy fellow who deliberately added a layer of dullness over the bright paints after the plaster dried. In their view, the solvents are removing not only soot and smoke, but part of the original artwork. So we are now seeing colors the artist did not intend us to see.

Well, maybe he wasn't so gloomy. I'm no expert, but I prefer the new Michelangelo.

It is officially spring now. Here and there we see a drop of primary color in a gray timescape. A cardinal. A crocus. A momentary flood of bright light. Soon the sun will drive the dullness away and the greenness and blueness and yellowness of the earth and the sky will spread out all around us.

I wonder if I am ready for spring within myself. I think I have some residue to clean away, deposited by the candles burned through long nights. I think I know what the solvents are: sunlight, children, music, prayer, true meetings with people, hands to hold.

Balancing Act

The minister finished his last editing pass through the sermon and told the computer to print it. He brushed his teeth and put on his tie. He noticed that he was later than usual. In less than twenty minutes 150 people would expect to see him climb into the pulpit and call them to worship.

He tore the printed sermon off and zipped it (along with the opening words, the children's story, the minister's prayer, and the benediction) into his briefcase and headed for the door. It being a sunny morning, he decided not to reach for his topcoat as he passed the hall closet. He heard the front door close behind him and remembered that his keys were in the coat pocket.

He circled the house checking the doors, which were all properly locked. He paused before the little-used side entrance with its latched storm door. Imagining himself in a movie, he broke a small pane of glass with his black-suited elbow and reached through to grasp the knob of the main door. It would not turn. (Two hours later he would walk home to find a police car in the driveway. Someone tried to break in, his wife would say.)

He set off briskly on the three-tenths mile walk to the church. He thought, 'These passing motorists must know who I am and how ridiculous this is.' (An hour later, two separate parishioners would tell him they almost stopped but thought he was walking for the exercise.)

As he breathlessly entered the parish house, an usher asked him where the books with the responsive readings were. They were locked in his office, along with his robe. He tried without success to find someone with a key to the secretary's desk, in which there was a key to his office. He decided he would go out without the robe and substitute a reading from another book.

He stood outside his office door tearing the perforated strips off the edges of his sermon. Someone came by with a key.

36

He opened the door, handed the carton of books to the usher, and sent a messenger to tell the organist to keep playing.

At eight minutes past, the robed minister entered the sanctuary smiling. He thought, 'I look like I'm OK.' He preached a good sermon about finding balance in our lives.

Easter Week 1982

The light green shoots of blossoms-to-have-been are out of sight under the drifting snow. Gale force winds are rattling the old house. The temperature is far below freezing. Nature is not cooperating with preparations for Easter.

The storm evokes the spiritual quality of Good Friday more than Easter. New life will appear, but not without strife, not without some losses to the coldness which returns as inevitably as spring. And who can say that the sun will always climb again on Easter morning? Isn't it at least possible that the coldness has more staying power than the warmth?

The seasons are more reliable in these matters than human nature. For we, individually and collectively, can choose between love and indifference, between commitment and self-absorption, between peace and war. And we have often chosen the coldness.

Maybe the ancients were right. Maybe the spring comes because we bid it to come in our celebrations. Maybe it is the telling and the retelling of the stories that enable us to see that hope still lives and that we can carry it forward.

The stories make it clear that God does not do it alone. The motions of the spheres will produce a sunrise, but the springtime of the spirit, the springtime of love and justice and peace, depends on our human response to the gift of life.

Let us tell the stories again.

Invocation for a Town Meeting
Called to Consider Aerial Spraying
to Control Gypsy Moths

Eternal God, mysterious source of life, who makest the mighty beast, the stately tree, the lowly insect, and the invisible virus, we assemble tonight to consider the destruction of some of thy creatures that others might live more abundantly.

Grant us humility before the wondrous complexity of the creation, the full mystery of which will never be revealed to human eyes.

Grant us wisdom as we take up our God-given powers to alter nature, that the deeds we do may not be ultimately destructive but rather in harmony with the creative spirit.

And grant us courage, though our knowledge is incomplete and our understanding imperfect, to go ahead and do the best we can.

The Divine Secret

Silence came before creation, and the heavens were spread without a word.

—James Martineau

Become a silent witness, without show
Or sensuality or selfishness;
Release all fond attachments; peel away
The layered thoughts until the inmost depth
Is reached; recall how short a time since you
Were not, how short a time again until
You will not be. Look on the quiet night's
Progression; see the ancient light of stars;
Recall how meager is the knowledge you
Can ever claim beyond the mystery
Of life and the persistence of its Source.

Then you may feel a presence, close as if
The night breeze brushing on your cheek were breath
Of the Creator; you may say, "Oh God,
Have you been always near as this without
My knowing you?" and you may see the depth
Of life revealed to show how little your
Temptations and how great your newfound trust.

Then you may be ashamed at your fatigue
Under so light a burden, and your tears
At such a petty trial. You may be
Astonished at how little dust has been

Required to block your vision. You may see
With sorrow all the jealousies and fears
That keep your life from being what it can.

A mighty wind of transformation will arise
To sweep away the musty atmosphere
About your soul until in freshness all
The flakes of difficulty melt like snow
Upon the sea. No longer trapped in time
You live in an eternity of now
And here. No longer separate, your soul
Is merged with all that ever lived to be
A wave upon the boundless sea of being.
You are one with all creation. You
Have found the secret place of the divine.

Surprised By Love

A funeral director in a nearby town called to ask if I would do a graveside service. It was for a man named Melvin.

I interviewed Melvin's cousin on the phone. Melvin had worked in a landscaping business belonging to another cousin. He was good with the plants and the soil, but not very good with money or with people. His mother left him her house, and he lived there alone until it got to be such a mess that it was uninhabitable. Then a few years ago he moved to Leominster, where he lived with a family who owned a motel. He was their handy man and helped take care of their kids. "That was odd," the cousin said, "because my kids couldn't stand him."

I called a man who worked with Melvin. He told a similar story. "I don't know what you could say," he admitted. "There probably won't be many people there."

It seemed Melvin's life had been a problem. It sounded as if these people were just going through the motions of having a service.

I got out the usual text I use for such occasions. The opening words and the prayer spoke of a person who was loved, and of survivors mourning their loss. I thought, these words would not be true for these people. They would know that I was only reading stock lines.

So where I usually say, "We have come here because someone we knew and loved has died; we are forever less because he has gone," I substituted, "We have come here because someone we knew has died."

And where I usually say, "We rejoice in his life and give thanks that we have walked the way with such a companion," I substituted, "We give thanks for his life."

There were about a dozen people at the grave site. I was asked to wait for some latecomers. At ten minutes past the hour a car pulled up. A woman and two teenagers got out. When the funeral director motioned the people to gather near the grave, the latecomers stood in front of the others.

As I began my laundered remarks the three of them started to weep. Large tears rolled down. They sobbed.

When it was over I spoke to one of the red-eyed teenagers. This was the family from Leominster. She told me how Melvin had lived in their house and cared for them, and then how the roles reversed. She told of his long illness, how she had taken food and medicine to his room when he was in pain and could barely swallow. And she told me of the day she had found him dead. She loved him. She began to cry again.

None of the people knew about the words I did not say. Several of them thanked me for the service, and I believe all of them were satisfied with it. But I was not satisfied. I was taken by surprise. I had prepared myself to meet indifference, but love showed up instead.

I am going to try never again to assume that any person is not loved. I am going to try to prepare for love.

Maybe today I will notice a spark of love in someone's heart. Maybe this time I will not be surprised.

Quite a Pickle

A person has died who was very dear to me. Her cancer was diagnosed four months earlier. There was an operation and then a long wait for the results of a biopsy. The news came and it was unambiguous: she had a terminal illness that was not treatable.

I knew her as a marvelously cheerful person. I expected that her response to her condition would be to keep smiling and change the subject. She did this for a while, but then one day she said to me, "This is quite a pickle I'm in." We talked about the pickle she was in. She told me what she had decided to do. She said, "I'm going to make the most of every day."

She did that. She spent her last weeks at home. She talked with her husband and children and grandchildren and friends. She enjoyed flowers and music. On the last day of her life she said goodbye to the people she loved most.

She reminded me of something I often forget: we are all in quite a pickle. We should be making the most of every day.

Memorial Day

O God, we are often bewildered as we seek to understand what it means to be alive and human in this world. We know we are capable of great selflessness, of great sacrifice. We may even lay down our lives for our fellow human beings, or for high principles. But we are also capable of great folly. We are capable of paying too great a price in human suffering and lives lost for ends which are too small.

As long as there is evil in this world, good people will be called upon to oppose it as best they can. Sometimes good people will conclude that they must send young men and women to kill, and to be killed. May we find, somehow, in the heat of particular circumstance, the wisdom to know when truly transcendent values are at stake, and the courage never to place precious human life at risk for the sake of pride, or greed, or political advantage.

On this Memorial Day we remember the many lives we have lost in military conflict in the history of our nation, from the Battle of Lexington to the Persian Gulf War. May we honor their memory by making a commitment of our lives, today, toward the creation of a new world—a world of justice and mercy, of forgiveness and reconciliation. A world in which our swords will be beaten into plowshares, our missiles and helicopter gunships made into schoolrooms and subway cars, our soldiers transformed into teachers and nurses and poets. A world in which we will make war no longer.

Shadow and Light

A nurse came into the Tennessee hospital room where I was visiting an old friend. My friend introduced us. "Well," said the nurse, upon hearing that I am a minister, "see what you think of this."

She took an object from her pocket, unwrapped it from several layers of plastic film, and handed it to me. It was a photograph. She explained that a friend of hers wanted a picture of Hurricane Hugo; he had gone out toward the end of the storm and taken a snapshot.

The picture showed a dark area of sky and some white clouds. She said, "What do you think of that?"

I searched for something of interest in the picture. I said, gamely, "It looks a little like Pac-Man." She said, "Look in the upper right corner."

I looked in the upper right corner and still saw nothing but clouds and sky. I thought, this hurricane caused immense destruction; maybe she sees a source of evil in these clouds. I looked for horns or a pitchfork or a pointy tail. Fortunately, I made no comment until she spoke again.

"It's Christ," she said.

She pointed. "There's his hand. There's his robe. . . ." Then the shape emerged and I saw what she wanted me to see. I acknowledged to her that I could now see it.

She said, "Well, what do you think of that?" Still not knowing what was expected of me, I said nothing. She said, "It's like he's pointing and saying, 'See what I can do?'" I said, "Hmm."

The nurse took the picture back, wrapped it in the plastic, pocketed it, and repeated, "It's like he's saying, 'See what I can do?'" She left the room.

She and I looked at the same pattern of shadow and light. She saw a vision of power in the hands of a figure of healing and forgiveness. I saw a vision of power that was chaotic and destructive—and that set me looking for the source of evil.

We were each grasping a part of the truth.

Interruption

On US-30, west of Gettysburg, I saw a dead deer beside the road. I sped on past. I had hundreds of miles to go that day. Then I felt called back. I made a U-turn on the four-lane highway and returned to the deer.

It was early on a Sunday morning. There was little traffic.

I approached and crouched beside the body. His eyes were open. I imagined for a moment that he was still alive, but there was no movement, no breath. I had been drawn to the deer by reverence and awe, but these gave way initially to curiosity and amateur forensic analysis.

One of his hind legs was broken, with the bone sticking out. There was a pool of dark blood under his head. There was a trail of blood about thirty feet long from the near lane of the highway. There were bony stubs where his antlers had been. I guessed he had been hit by a car, had died of a head injury, and had been dragged by someone to the shoulder of the road. I guessed the antlers had been taken for souvenirs.

I touched his side, his face, his broken leg. I sat with him for a minute or two, then decided to move him off the shoulder and into the underbrush. I pulled him by his forelegs, dragging him over and down a six-foot bank. I covered him with large leaves of weeds that grew there.

I said a prayer. I apologized for the system, my system, of people and machines and roads that had brought his meaningless death. I apologized for the indifference, which I have shared, that had brought his mutilation. I gave thanks for having found the courage to stop and to touch him.

I returned to my car and resumed my journey south.

The Sniper at Hall's Corner

A priest who for two years has been in a struggle with cancer told me how that struggle has changed his life. There are things that used to bother him to which he now pays no attention. He has turned loose of his need to control everything in the parish. Now among the many demands on his time he easily chooses the important ones and says no to the others.

I asked him: Why has your close encounter with death made a difference? You were going to die anyway, even if you had not gotten cancer. I am going to die, and I know it; yet I still waste time on trivia, and worry about what I can't change, and try to control what does not need my control. We risk death every time we drive down to Hall's Corner, yet how many of us are making the best of each day?

He said: You know you are going to die, but you don't *believe* it the way I do. If you knew there was a sniper waiting at Hall's Corner it would add meaning to the statement, "Honey, I'm going down to the post office."

What I want is balance. I want enough awareness of death to remind me of the gift of this day, but also enough distance from death to be able to concentrate on this day.

Give me an occasional glimpse of mortality: a falling leaf, the burial of a pet, a news report of a death far away. Spare me for now the close encounter: the death of a close friend, the sharp pain in the chest, the sound of a rifle shot.

I don't want to go around all the time thinking I am in someone's cross hairs. And yet, it may only be when that bullet hits the sidewalk next to me that I will know what my friend the priest knows.

The One Truth

I pray that for you there may be moments, perhaps minutes or even hours, of a larger awareness, a seeing through surfaces to essence.

Everything around you is a manifestation of a reality that is a unity.

It is there in the maple tree, in the polished beach stone, in the cumulus cloud.

It is there in the tilled soil, the clapboard siding, the comfortable chair.

It is in the child's laugh, the worker's sweat, your face in the mirror.

It is in the fear of war, the anger at injustice, the longing for love, the commitment to reconciliation.

The many truths spring from the one truth, and the beginning of wisdom is to open ourselves to the mystery of the one truth. May the moments of awareness be there in your days, and in mine, too.

Unitarian and Universalist
Meditation Manuals

Unitarians and Universalists have been publishing annual editions of prayer collections and meditation manuals for 150 years. In 1841 the Unitarians broke with their tradition of addressing only theological topics and published *Short Prayers for the Morning and Evening of Every Day in the Week, with Occasional Prayers and Thanksgivings*. Over the years, the Unitarians published many volumes of prayers, including Theodore Parker's selections. In 1938 *Gaining a Radiant Faith* by Henry H. Saunderson launched the current tradition of an annual Lenten manual.

Several Universalist collections appeared in the early nineteenth century. A comprehensive *Book of Prayers* was published in 1839, featuring both public and private devotions. During the late 1860s, the Universalist Publishing House was founded to publish denominational materials. Like the Unitarians, the Universalists published Lenten manuals, and in the 1950s they complemented this series with Advent manuals.

Since 1961, the year the Unitarians and the Universalists merged, the Lenten manual has evolved into a meditation manual, reflecting the theological diversity of the two denominations. Today the Unitarian Universalist Association meditation manuals include two styles of collections: poems or short prose pieces written by one author—usually a Unitarian Universalist minister—and anthologies of works by many authors.

The following list includes all meditation manuals since the merger, plus several titles prior to 1961. Currently, there is no definitive list of Universalist titles published before 1961.

1991　*Been in the Storm So Long*　Mark Morrison-Reed and Jacqui James, Editors[‡]

1990　*Into the Wilderness*　Sara Moores Campbell[‡]

1989   *A Small Heaven* Jane Ranney Rzepka[‡]

1988   *The Numbering of Our Days* Anthony Friess Perrino[‡]

1987   *Exaltation* David B. Parke, Editor[‡]

1986   *Quest* Kathy Fuson Hurt[‡]

1985   *The Gift of the Ordinary*   Charles S. Stephen, Jr., Editor

1984   *To Meet the Asking Years* Gordon B. McKeeman, Editor[‡]

1983   *Tree and Jubilee* Greta W. Crosby

1981   *Outstretched Wings of the Spirit* Donald S. Harrington[‡]

1980   *Longing of the Heart* Paul N. Carnes

1979   *Portraits From the Cross* David Rankin

1978   *Songs of Simple Thanksgiving* Kenneth L. Patton

1977   *The Promise of Spring* Clinton Lee Scott

1976   *The Strangeness of This Business* Clarke D. Wells

1975   *In Unbroken Line* Chris Raible, Editor

1974   *Stopping Places* Mary Lou Thompson

1973   *The Tides of Spring* Charles W. Grady

1972   *73 Voices* Chris Raible and Ed Darling, Editors

1971   *Bhakti, Santi, Love, Peace* Jacob Trapp

1970   *Beginning Now* J. Donald Johnston

1969   *Answers in the Wind* Charles W. McGehee

1968   *The Trying Out* Richard Kellaway

1967   *Moments of Springtime* Rudolf Nemser

1966   *Across the Abyss* Walter D. Kring

1965   *The Sound of Silence* Raymond Baughan

1964   *Impassioned Clay* Ralph Helverson

1963   *Seasons of the Soul* Robert T. Weston

1962   *The Uncarven Image* Phillip Hewett

1961   *Parts and Proportions* Arthur Graham

1960   *Imprints of the Divine* Raymond Hopkins

1959   *Indictments and Invitations* Robert B. Cope

1958   *Strange Beauty* Vincent Silliman

1957   *Greatly to Be* Francis Anderson, Jr.

1956   *My Heart Leaps Up* Frank O. Holmes

1955   *The Task Is Peace* Harry Scholefield

1954 *Taking Down the Defenses* Arthur Foote
1953 *My Ample Creed* Palfrey Perkins
1952 *This Man Jesus* Harry C. Meserve
1951 *The Tangent of Eternity* John Wallace Laws
1950 *Deep Sources and Great Becoming* Edwin C. Palmer
1949 *To Take Life Strivingly* Robert Killan
1948 *Come Up Higher* Hurley Begun
1947 *Untitled* Richard Steiner
1946 *The Pattern on the Mountain* (reissue) E. Burdette Backus
1945 *The Expendable Life* Charles G. Girelius
1944 *The Disciplines of Freedom* Leslie T. Pennington
1943 *Faith Forbids Fear* Frederick May Eliot
1942 *Forward into the Light* Frederick W. Griffin
1941 *Victorious Living* W. W. W. Argow
1940 *Address to the Living* Herbert Hitchen
1939 *The Pattern on the Mountain* E. Burdette Backus
1938 *Gaining a Radiant Faith* Henry H. Saunderson

‡ These meditation manuals are available from the Unitarian Universalist Association. For a free catalog, write to the UUA Bookstore, 25 Beacon St., Boston, MA 02108-2800.

About the Author

Since 1980, Robert Rea Walsh has been minister of the First Parish Church, Unitarian Universalist, in Duxbury, Massachusetts. He has also served on the boards of the Unitarian Universalist Association and the Unitarian Universalist Service Committee.

Raised in Kingsport, Tennessee, he holds degrees from the Massachusetts Institute of Technology and Harvard Divinity School. Before entering the professional ministry, he had a career in industrial management. He can play the five-string banjo. He and his wife, Reed, have three children—Elizabeth, David, and Nathaniel.